"WHEN I SAW HIM...
where revival begins

"WHEN I SAW HIM..."
where revival begins

by
ROY HESSION

CHRISTIAN LITERATURE CRUSADE
Fort Washington, Pennsylvania 19034

CHRISTIAN LITERATURE CRUSADE
U.S.A.
Box 1449, Fort Washington, PA 19034

Copyright©1975
Christian Literature Crusade
Fort Washington, PA

This printing 1988

ISBN 0-87508-239-4

PRINTED IN THE UNITED STATES OF AMERICA

"When I saw Him,
I fell at His feet as dead."

—Revelation 1:17

CONTENTS

FOREWORD

I first met Roy in the summer of 1926 when I had been asked to lead a holiday houseparty for older schoolboys at the seaside mission at Southwold on the east coast of England. I had rarely seen such a collection of youthful enthusiasts. Every day we would think of some new escapade, and one of these was a swim around the Southwold pier. (It was twice as long as it is today.) All fifteen boys would change in our big house on the seafront and then, led by Roy, who was just eighteen, and his younger brother Brian, would rush for the sea. It was Roy, with his professional crawl, who would lead the way swimming around the pier.

In our morning and evening prayers the Bible lit up as we saw "the Captain of the Host" appearing to Joshua, and the One who called His disciples beside the Lake of Galilee. In faith we asked God that each one of those fifteen boys would answer the call to follow Him, and to the glory of God we believe every one of them did so personally, led by Roy and Brian, who never looked back. Roy seemed to take me as an elder brother, and that friendship has deepened and grown as the years have gone by.

After that time, for the next twenty years we went our various ways without seeing one another; Roy into a London bank and then into full-time evangelistic service; and I into life as a medical missionary in East Africa, coming home on leave every four years to tell of a deep movement of revival which God had graciously allowed us to experience—both the Africans and us missionaries. In 1947 a small team of us had come home with the definite vision of sharing with the Christians of England what we had been learning in revival in East Africa. A telephone call from Roy linked us up again after all those years and resulted in the team being invited to the Bible conference houseparty which Roy was running at Matlock, in the center of England. The messages, fresh from a convention in Western Uganda, were given, and afterwards were written up by Roy in his book *The Calvary Road,* which also contained other chapters expressive of the new experience of Jesus that he and others in England were finding. From that time it began to go on its way round the world, reaching more than half a million copies in English alone, as well as various editions in other languages.

That same message has sent us, sometimes together, not around the pier, but around far-off parts of the world with the message of revival to North America, Brazil, India, Europe, and Africa, where the winds of the Holy Spirit have been blowing. Roy's enthusiasm is always infectious, and everywhere there are left behind those who have caught the vision.

Now in 1974 Roy and I have found ourselves together again, at the fifteenth revival convention in Leysin, Switzerland, and as he feels guided to write up the messages he gave there, he has asked me to write a foreword to this new book of his.

I praise God for every memory of what He has done through Roy and his books, and I recommend those who read this one to listen to the voice of the Holy Spirit calling us all to see the vision again of the glorified Lord moving "in the midst of the candlesticks," and to be given again our "first love" to go all out for revival.

May God send this message out with His blessing around the world. The promise still stands in 2 Chronicles 7:14:

> If My people, which are called by My Name, shall humble themselves, and pray, and seek My face, and turn from their wicked ways; then will I hear from heaven, and will forgive their sin, and will heal their land.

JOE CHURCH, M.A., M.R.C.S.

Little Shelford,
Cambridge,
July, 1974

1

"WHEN I SAW HIM. . . ."

In the opening chapters of the Book of Revelation the Apostle John tells us how on the Isle of Patmos he was given an awesome vision of the Lord Jesus, risen from the dead. It was a full-length portrait of Him as He is right now, in deeply symbolic terms, of course. His head and His hair were as white as snow, His eyes like a flame of fire, His feet like burnished bronze glowing as if in a furnace, His voice as the sound of many waters, His right hand holding seven stars, from His mouth proceeding a sharp two-edged sword and His whole countenance shining as the sun in full strength. Then John says, "When I saw Him, I fell at His feet as dead." He tells us not only the vision itself, but the profound effect it had on him. It utterly prostrated him before the Lord until He came and laid His right hand on him and said "Fear not."

The subject of this little book is "When I saw Him. . . ." Notice these words carefully. They speak not only about seeing Him, but the effect that a vision of Him has upon us. Those who have not seen such a vision will not understand what is happening to those who have. They will see certain effects taking place in them, but will not realize what has caused them. They will be puzzled to see them often repenting, often "falling down at His feet as dead," and yet all the time praising Him and full of joy. To them continual repentance and continual joy had always seemed to be mutually exclusive. But when they have seen the vision of the Lord themselves, they will be doing the very same things and will be able to say "Now I understand! I am seeing what they are seeing and what I see is having the same effect on me."

In the following pages I invite the reader to look with me at four men of old (in one of the cases in question, a group of men) who saw the Lord, and at the effects the visions had on them. I do so because the particular revelations of the Lord they had are the same revelations of Him we need, and when we have them they will have the same effect on us as they had on them.

Let it be said here that no one of these studies is going to give us the whole picture. They will take us aspect by aspect through the truth and we will not see the whole picture till towards the end. I want you therefore to resist the temptation of saying that the message is so negative, or so something else, until you have read the whole. So often when we read a book we omit the last chapters, thinking that we have got its message from the earlier ones. I beg you not to do this as you may find the last part of the book the most vital part for you. Of course, not even by the end of this little book will the message be complete; we will have to wait till glory for that!

My hope and prayer is that the reader will not only read about these people having a vision of the Lord, but that as he peruses these pages the Holy Spirit will actually give him a similar vision. It is important therefore that he should not think that he knows it all. He may indeed know much about the message of revival and he may not find any new thing in these pages. As I see it, what the Lord desires to do is to take us all much deeper in what we already know and give us a much deeper conviction of sin and brokenness than we have ever experienced before and with regard to areas we have never allowed Him to touch before. It might be His purpose for these pages to be stained with the tears of the one who reads them, as he looks again on Him whom he has pierced and mourns for Him, and as a result be brought into an altogether new liberty and fruitfulness.

This is the stuff of which revival is made, as I have known it come to my own life and that of many others. I use the word "it" quite deliberately, because so many children of God are seeking an "it" as the answer to their own need and that of the church, an "it" which they have not as yet found. And they never will, until they see Jesus coming to them across the waves and saying, "Fear not, 'it' is I." Revival in its essence is nothing more than our finding Jesus again after having long struggled in other directions for the answer and at last finding Him—not by some higher attainment, but by taking the place of sinners again.

In the year that King Uzziah died, I saw also the Lord sitting upon a throne, high and lifted up, and His train filled the temple. Above it stood the seraphim: each one had six wings; with two he covered his face, and with two he covered his feet, and with two he did fly. And one cried unto another, and said, Holy, holy, holy, is the Lord of hosts; the whole earth is full of His glory. And the posts of the door moved at the voice of him who cried, and the house was filled with smoke.

Then said I, Woe is me! For I am undone, because I am a man of unclean lips, and I dwell in the midst of a people of unclean lips; for mine eyes have seen the King, the Lord of hosts.

Then flew one of the seraphim unto me, having a live coal in his hand, which he had taken with the tongs from off the altar. And he laid it upon my mouth, and said, Lo, this hath touched thy lips and thine iniquity is taken away, and thy sin purged.

Also I heard the voice of the Lord, saying, Whom shall I send, and who will go for us? Then said I, Here am I; send me. And He said, Go.

Isaiah 6:1–9

2

WHEN ISAIAH SAW HIM.

The Vision of the Throne.

In the sixth chapter of his prophecy Isaiah tells us how he was given a vision of the Lord and about the profound effect it had upon him. His life was never the same afterwards and he was given an entirely new ministry.

The interesting thing is that this man was a preacher before he ever had this vision. Indeed, we have five chapters of his sermons before he saw the Lord in this way. It is apparently only in chapter six that he sees the Lord, high and lifted up. What was he doing all those years of preaching before he had this vision? He was working for God and doubtless doing so very hard, but without vision. What a terrible possibility for us to be very busy in our service for God, but without vision, or at least without a new vision—serving only in the strength of an old one that has become stale. This is something very prevalent in Christian service at home and on the mission field, where many are working for God but without a new personal vision of Him. The work as a result becomes heavy. There is little outcome from it. And the worker himself becomes utterly discouraged. But he knows nothing better and he plods on, not seeing that he does not see. But there came a day when Isaiah did see, when God granted him a new vision of Himself. Wonderful day for Isaiah!

We can see what the emphasis of his message was during those early years by glancing through his first five chapters. There are scattered throughout it constant woes pronounced on evil-doers: "Woe unto you that do this. . . . Woe unto you that do the other"; there are six such woes. Truly his message is important, but there is no woe pronounced on himself. It is not until chapter 6, when he sees the Lord high and lifted up, that he says, "Woe is me! For I am undone . . . mine eyes have seen the King." All those years he had been working not only without vision but without a broken spirit, pointing the finger at others, condemning others, but not seeing himself. We can be doing the same, criticizing others, pronouncing woes on others, without having been humbled to say, "Woe is me! For I am undone"—and that because we have not seen what Isaiah saw. As a result revival has not yet begun in our hearts, for the Lord is only near those of a broken and contrite spirit, "to revive the spirit of the humble, and to revive the heart of the contrite ones."[1]

I want you to notice the occasion of his vision of the Lord. He tells us that it happened in the year that

1. Isa. 57:15.

King Uzziah died. The story of that king is given in 2 Chronicles 26. He was a God-fearing king and as long as he sought the Lord, God made him to prosper. He was marvelously helped in all his enterprises until he was strong. But when he was strong, his heart was lifted up in pride to his destruction and he took it upon himself to offer incense in the holy place of the temple, something that only the priests were permitted to do. The priests tried to withstand him, saying "This is transgressing the commandment of God," but he went in with his censer. And as they looked at him, they saw a white patch appear on his forehead. They all knew what it was; it was leprosy. God had smitten him that day for his sin, and though he hasted to get out of the holy place he was a leper until the day of his death, living in a separate house. And it was in the year that he died that Isaiah saw the Lord, high and lifted up. Having seen how God would judge even a king for his sin, Isaiah saw what a holy God he had to deal with.

The occasion of our seeing the Lord will vary. Something may happen that will precipitate a crisis and we shall find ourselves standing before God in a new way. It could be something like that which shook Isaiah. That is how it was in the church at Ephesus in Acts 19. A new vision of God came to the Ephesian church when they saw how God confounded those Jewish exorcists who took it upon themselves to cast out demons in the name of Jesus. They did not cast out the demon at all, but the man in whom the demon was leapt on them and they had to flee. And when the church saw it, they saw they were dealing with a holy God and that no man could trifle with the name of Jesus. They began to see sin in their own lives, for they themselves had been playing with the occult and black magic, and a great spirit of repentance swept the church. They brought out their hidden things of darkness and burnt them openly.

Sometimes it is some special occasion of the judgment of sin like this that makes the saints see the Lord again. Years ago I met a man and his wife who had a wonderful ministry of sharing Jesus as a team of two all over their area, and he told me how it all started. He was an elder in a Presbyterian church and their minister was overtaken in a moral fault. It shocked the church and the elders who had to deal with it, and they had to ask the minister to leave. He said that it was in the year that that scandal broke upon the church that he himself saw the Lord, how holy He was, and he saw his own sins in the light of that holiness. "I might not have done exactly what my pastor had done," he said, "but in God's sight I saw sin just as bad as his. I had things to put right with my wife and others, and I entered into a new experience of victory in Christ." God can use even scandal to wake up the saints. When we see how God judges sin in others, His searchlight is turned on us. However, the variety of things God uses is infinite.

What did Isaiah see? He saw the Lord, high and lifted up, sitting upon a throne. Around the throne there were seraphim—beautiful creatures, scintillating with light—whose constant task was to proclaim to one another the holiness and glory of the One upon the throne. As they did so the temple was shaken to its foundations—and Isaiah shook with them—and the temple was filled with smoke. This was the cloud that from time to time appeared in Israel's history, symbolizing the presence and glory of God and called the "Shekinah" cloud of glory. When that cloud filled the newly erected tabernacle in the wilderness Moses was unable to enter because of it. When centuries later the temple was built in Jerusalem the same "Shekinah" cloud of glory filled it to show that God was there, and the priests could not stand to minister because of it. And here was poor Isaiah having to remain gazing on it all.

It was, however, the action of the awesome seraphim that seems to have broken him down especially. Such was the holiness of God, they were veiling themselves before Him. Each of them had six wings; with two of them they hid their faces, with two of them they hid their feet, and with only two of them they flew. Four of their six wings were used to hide themselves before the face of the One upon the throne. Why were they doing this? Because although they were beautiful, the One upon the throne was infinitely more so, and they were concerned lest in any degree their beauty should somehow divert attention from that other Beauty. So they made it their supreme task to hide themselves with four of their wings that only the Lord on the throne might be seen; only two of their six wings were used for service. This sight, I imagine, had a profound effect on Isaiah. In the light of the action of those creatures, greater in power and might than ever he could be, whose supreme concern was to hide themselves before God, he saw that his supreme concern had been to display himself. I take it that his attitude up till then had in effect been, "If I am gifted by God, if I have a call from God, if I am working for God, then others should see!" He was not using any wings to hide himself. He had been working hard on all six wings and hoping people would see it all. Sure, he had been doing it all for God, but there were all sorts of extra bonuses that had come his way because of it—bonuses by way of status and the praise of men—and, we can guess, he secretly enjoyed them and had allowed them to become the motivation of much of what he was doing. Now as he looked upon all that was happening before the throne of God he came under terrible conviction of sin, the realization that his service was self-inspired, and in complete brokenness he cried out "Woe is me! For I am undone!"

Listen as he continues and gives us the reason for this woe he pronounces upon himself: ". . . because I am a man of unclean lips." What did he mean by this expression? The lips are the tools of the heart, and if his lips were unclean it was because his heart was unclean. More than that, his lips represented his service: he was a preacher. If there was one part of him he thought was consecrated to God, it was his lips; he had golden lips, gifted lips. But that day he saw that even his consecrated service was unclean and unacceptable to God because it was all self-inspired. He would never have seen this had his eyes not looked upon the King, the Lord of hosts, and the seraphim hiding themselves before Him. It was a revelation of God, as it has to be for us.

This sort of scene is going on in heaven at this very moment. We must not think that this scene was laid on just for Isaiah's benefit. When we turn to Revelation, chapter four, we see the same thing happening, centuries afterwards. John sees the same throne, the same One upon it, the same heavenly creatures, and hears a similar cry, "Holy, holy, holy, Lord God Almighty, who was, and is, and is to come."[2] This had been going on in heaven all the time and continues

2. Rev. 4:8.

there to this very hour. The seraphim are still proclaiming the holiness and glory of God, and they are still hiding themselves before Him. God wants us to see what Isaiah saw, that <u>our supreme concern has been to display self</u> and even to use our service for God to that end. Though it is His work we are engaged in, <u>the underlying motive has been</u> "<u>be seen, be known, be heard.</u>" This is a terrible sin in the eyes of God and should be so too in our eyes; the pride of it, the rebellion of it, abusing the grace of God and our call to service in order that we should be displayed and get the glory, and in so doing hiding the glory of the One we profess to be serving.

A former generation of Christians knew well the name of Mrs. Penn-Lewis. She was much involved in the great Welsh revival at the beginning of this century. In one of her books she tells how God dealt with her. One day she had a vision in which it seemed God was holding up before her a bundle of filthy rags. She said to God, "What is that, Lord?" and He said, "It is your service, My child." "But," she said, "it is consecrated service." "Yes," He said, "consecrated flesh." <u>Our service</u> can just be flesh; that is, the natural, fallen self, consecrated to God—and God does not want it consecrated to Him. It is <u>full of wrong motives</u>. He Himself has described the mind of the flesh as enmity against Himself.[3] He has judged that flesh at the cross of Jesus, where His Son was made in its likeness and was judged as it. Rather than consecrate it to Him, He wants us to accept His judgment of it, in order that the life of the Lord Jesus might be manifest in us.

What did Isaiah mean when he said, "For I am undone"? It is a deep word. I think it means he

3. Rom. 8:7.

saw that the thing with which he had previously been content in himself had all the time been abomination in the sight of God; that what he had always regarded as gain was in reality dead loss. This must have been a shocking experience for Isaiah, as it is for us, when after years of apparently successful service we see in the light of God that much of it, if not all, has been done in the strength of the flesh and for the glory of self; that it has just been *our* work for Him rather than *His* work through us, and that the Lord Himself has not been the center of it. Then indeed "our comeliness is turned into corruption," as was Daniel's when he saw the Lord.[4] I remember Dr. Joe Church said to me when he returned to England (as he mentions in his foreword): "I find the Christians in England have the queerest idea of what revival is. They think it is the top blowing off, when in reality it is the bottom falling out!" I laughed at the time, but I little knew how soon after God would indeed cause the bottom to fall out of what I thought was my consecrated Christian service and that I would begin to say, "Woe is me, for I am undone." I seemed to lose all my confidence as a preacher and hardly knew what to preach or how to do it, until I learned again the message of God's grace for sinners and saw a deeper meaning in the blood of Jesus and its power to cleanse than I had before.

This, then, is the conviction of sin corresponding to Isaiah's that God desires to give us as we see Him in His holiness: that our service has been done in the flesh, perhaps for many years, and that without our knowing it. Self has intruded even into holy things, and so much of what has been done has been only in

4. Dan. 10:8.

the power of the self-life rather than in the power of the Holy Spirit.

I want to stay longer on this all-important matter of the intrusion of self into our Christian lives and service. I think we can say there are three main forms of the self-life. First of all, there is *self-will*—I make the plans; I, rather than the Lord, initiate things. As each day dawns, I am the king of that day and if I want to indulge in something, I will.

The second form of the self-life is *self-effort*—I trying to do God's work for Him by my own efforts, expedients, and schemes. And, of course, this follows from the first. What begins *with* me, has to be done *by* me. This applies not only to service, but to the Christian life itself. He says, "I thought you understood that the Christian life was My responsibility in you, but you are making your promises and trying to do better yourself." This, too, is the intrusion of self.

And then there is the third form of the self-life, *self-glory*—the desire for people to think well of us; the doing of things ostensibly for God, but really for our own glory, hoping that people will think "What a victorious Christian!" or "What a wonderful preacher!" or "What a great soul-winner!" or "What a beautiful Christian home!"

These, I suggest, are the main forms of the self-life. You can see them all in Nebuchadnezzar's proud words with regard to his capital city, Babylon. "Is not this great Babylon, that I have built"—self-will—"by the might of my power"—self-effort—"for the honor of my majesty?"—self-glory.[5] God's plan is completely otherwise. You have it in Romans 11:36:

5. Dan. 4:30.

". . . of Him, and through Him, and to Him, are all things." When we see the Lord we are convicted of this right down to details, in the holy as well as the secular part of our lives.

Sometimes we do not help one another in the way we speak. We say about a certain Christian worker, "God is blessing him in that town." What do we mean, God is blessing him? We mean that God is using him. But God is not blessing him so much as blessing the others to whom he ministers; He sees their need is so great that He will pick up a bit of rubbish like that man to help them. Do we not see the danger in speaking like this? We come to regard being used of God as a coveted prize. If we get it, we are proud and think it must be due to something in us. If we do not, we are disappointed in ourselves and jealous over others apparently more successful than we are, and struggle by our own efforts to obtain the prize next time. How terrible this all is! It is not a prize He is going to give to you; it is a prize He wants to give to those poor and needy people to whom He sends you. It is only His love for them that causes Him to take you up. There are many things He has to deal with you about; He is just waiting His time. Meanwhile He will use you, but in His own time He will show you Himself and you will see yourself more sinful than the very people you have been ministering to. And then you will no longer be trying to be a shepherd over sheep, but taking your place as a sheep among sheep, a sheep that has gone astray whom the Shepherd has restored, and you will share that with your fellow sheep.

Then the Lord has gone on to deal with me over self-effort. So often it has been me doing it and I find I cannot do it. How hard it all seems to be when I am trying to do it. If it were Jesus doing it it would be very different, but all too often it is me doing it.

And now, more recently, the Lord has been dealing with me over self-will, my self-initiated service, my attempts and schemes to bring revival to a wider circle. Having heard of mighty, widespread blessing in other countries, *I* decided we should have the same in England and *I* began to take means and measures to that end. But God has had to rebuke me for taking His place as the initiator of His work. There is, of course, a place for a right co-operation with God (more of that in another chapter), but He must be the initiator of the work and not us.

Oh, this terrible intrusion of self! It was because of this that Moses was excluded from the Promised Land. As he smote the rock twice (God had told him only to speak to it) he said, "Hear now, ye rebels, must we fetch you water out of this rock?"[6] The intrusion of self was seen here in more than one way. First, he adopted the attitude that their murmurings were against him, rather than against the Lord. On a previous occasion he had said, "Your murmurings are not against us, but against the Lord"[7]—but not this time. Previously in a situation like this he had fallen on his face before the Lord, but this time he stood on his feet with eyes blazing, having lost his temper with them.

Then secondly, he spoke as if he and Aaron were to bring the people water out of the rock: "Must *we* fetch you water out of this rock?" It was the Lord who

6. Num. 20:10.
7. Ex. 16:8.

was going to do it, not they. What a grievous intrusion of self to speak like this!

Then, thirdly, he acted as if simply to speak to the rock and let God do the rest was not enough; he had to *do* something about it, and something spectacular—and he smote the rock twice. Failing in faith, he acted in self-effort and self-will.

Then God spoke to him and told him that *he* was the rebel, not the people. Moses had called the people rebels, but when God spoke to him He said in effect, *You* rebelled against My word." The Lord went even deeper with him and said that in acting as he had, he had failed to (quoting the actual words) "sanctify Me in the eyes of the children of Israel";[8] that is, he had misrepresented God to the people. God wanted them to see Him as a long-suffering God, merciful and gracious, bearing patiently with their sin, and that the rock had only to be spoken to and water would be available for them. This would have done more to melt the people to repentance for their murmuring and unbelief than anything else. Moses, however, gave the impression that God was a resentful God, pointing His finger at them—something that would be more likely to harden them than otherwise. This was sin indeed, and so it was that Moses and Aaron were denied the culminating desire of their lives, that of leading the people into the long-promised land.

All this is a picture, point for point, of the way in which self has intruded into our Christian lives and service. We who are in any degree leaders have had those who have opposed us; but we have not fallen on our faces before the Lord and recognized that their opposition is not against us but against Him.

8. Num. 20:12.

We have rather reacted in a personal way, as if it were a personal affront to us, and in bitterness and anger have thought of them as "ye rebels." We have, perhaps, lain awake at night, having mental arguments with them—and have won every argument! And it has not been only *mental* arguments; words have followed thoughts, and sometimes eyes have flashed.

In so doing we, like Moses, have exalted ourselves as if *we* were in control, as if *we* were to bring them water out of the rock. We forgot that self cannot do anything—except fail—and we lost sight of Jesus. The attitudes we have adopted sometimes when disputed with have been truly blasphemous. What terrible words, "Must *we* fetch you water . . .?" What a grievous intrusion of self!

Then too, like Moses, we cannot believe that so little on our part as just speaking to the Rock can produce as big a result as is needed. We must *do* something, and do something *strong.* Failing in faith we act in the flesh—a further intrusion of self.

When God at last speaks to us it is to show that we who were calling other people rebels are ourselves the real rebels. We have rebelled against His way of gentleness and forgiveness and chosen our own way. And in doing so we have misrepresented Him and given an impression of Him quite other than the gracious God He is, and have hardened people rather than melted them. We need inquire no further as to why we seem to have been excluded from the promised land of a happy and victorious Christian life: we have not seen the intrusion of self in our situations and relationships with others; or seeing it, have not chosen deeply to repent of it.

And thus it was that Isaiah was broken in repentance and said, "Woe is me! I am undone; I am a man of unclean lips." "Then [and only then] flew one of the seraphim unto me." Here comes the gospel for the penitent soul. We will permit ourselves only a glimpse of it at this early stage in the book—much more will follow.

Can we imagine this contrite cry reaching the ears of those seraphim? Could we take the liberty of imagining one of them saying to another, "Did you hear something? It sounded like a sinner repenting. I heard 'Woe is me, for I am undone.' There is a man in distress down there. He has lost hope; he thinks there is no mercy for him." Could we picture him turning to God and saying, "O Lord of the throne, can you spare me for a moment?" and the Lord replying, "Go quickly to him; he needs all the comfort heaven can give him; for I will not contend forever, neither will I be always wroth. Go, lose not a moment." And the seraph goes to the altar. There is a lamb there, lying in the flames for just this situation, bearing the judgment of this man's sin. The seraph takes a live coal from off the altar, a token of the judgment finished there for him by the lamb. He flies to Isaiah and puts it upon his mouth, saying, "Lo, this hath touched thy lips, and thine iniquity is taken away, and thy sin purged." The Hebrew word translated "purged" is more literally "expiated." In using this word the seraph is in effect pointing back to the altar, saying, "Your sin has been expiated fully there."

There are two things here: "Your iniquity has been taken away"—something subjective—and "your sin expiated"—something objective. The subjective is based, as always, on the objective. His sin was taken away, and he could feel that it had been, because by faith he saw it had first been anticipated and expiated on the altar.

What a picture here of the altar of Calvary's cross, of the Lamb of God who was hung upon it and of the power of His precious blood. The Holy Spirit comes to us when we say "Woe is me" and points us back to the cross, telling us our sin has been anticipated and fully expiated by Jesus through His blood to the satisfaction of God, and the Spirit applies that blood to our unclean lips, meaning our carnal service and many sins, telling us they are taken away and the stain of them fully cleansed. We cannot be more right with God than what the blood makes us when we call sin, sin. We are now fully restored and able to respond to the call, "Whom shall I send, and who will go for us?" and hear the Lord say to us, "Go!" But this time, how different!

> No more let it be my working,
>   Nor my wisdom, love, or power,
> But the life of Jesus only,
>   Passing through me hour by hour.*

—F.H. Allen

If self intrudes again, and it may do so, we known exactly what to do and how to come into freedom again—back to His cross for cleansing. If in despair we say there, "Lord, I have done it again," He simply replies, "What have you done again?" There is just no record of it ever having happened before, because of the full cleansing of the blood of Jesus. If we see this way of the blood, we cannot but win and Satan and his accusations be overcome.

*From *Keswick Hymn Book*. Used by kind permission.

Have we anything hopeful to say of Moses here? The last we saw of him he was excluded from the Promised Land. If the grace of God reached Isaiah, could it not reach Moses? Indeed it could and did. First, it is clear that Moses repented and did so deeply. Remember, it was he who wrote the story of his sin, and no man says things like that about himself, excusing nothing, without having first humbled himself before God about it all. The story as we read it must be regarded as Moses' testimony. Second, grace reached him, for he got into the land after all and in a better way than he ever dreamed. When Jesus was transfigured before His disciples on that mount in Canaan, there is Moses standing with Him and Elijah. He has made the Promised Land after all! What a wonderful door of hope this shows there to be for any man who will cease to blame others and consent to say before God, "Woe is me." He too will find himself brought into the Promised Land of Blessing where all is forgiven and Jesus is really Lord.

And Saul, yet breathing out threatenings and slaughter against the disciples of the Lord, went unto the high priest, and desired of him letters to Damascus to the synagogues, that if he found any of this way, whether they were men or women, he might bring them bound unto Jerusalem.

And as he journeyed, he came near Damascus, and suddenly there shone round about him a light from heaven; and he fell to the earth, and heard a voice saying unto him, Saul, Saul, why persecutest thou Me?

And he said, Who art thou, Lord? And the Lord said, I am Jesus, whom thou persecutest; it is hard for thee to kick against the goads.

And he, trembling and astonished, said, Lord, what wilt Thou have me to do? And the Lord said unto him, Arise, and go into the city, and it shall be told thee what thou must do.

And the men who journeyed with him stood speechless, hearing a voice, but seeing no man.

And Saul arose from the earth, and when his eyes were opened, he saw no man; but they led him by the hand, and brought him into Damascus. And he was three days without sight, and neither did eat nor drink.

Acts 9:1–9

3

WHEN SAUL OF TARSUS SAW HIM.

The Vision of the Cross.

I only wish we could read the story opposite as if we had never read it before. It is an extraordinary story—you would have thought it extraordinary if it had happened to you—the story of how Saul of Tarsus, the self-righteous Pharisee, met the Lord on the road to Damascus and of the life-transforming effect it had on him.

He was the last person that people thought would have had a meeting with the Lord Jesus. The Christians could hardly believe it; neither could Saul of Tarsus. First of all, there was that great light from heaven that knocked him off his mule. Then out of that light there came a living voice. He knew he was being met by a supernatural Person. That was shock enough for Saul. And when that supernatural Person told him he was persecuting Him and then revealed His name as Jesus, it was more than he could bear.

Now what effect did this vision of Jesus have on Saul on the inside? We all know that it changed his whole life, but why? Saul was never slow in later years to tell about the effect of this vision on him. Paul was always giving his personal experience with regard to the matter. He gives his testimony on five occasions in the New Testament: twice in the Acts of the Apostles, then in his letter to the Galatians (chapters 1 and 2), then the story of his inner struggles in Romans 7, and then again, a really comprehensive testimony, in his letter to the Philippians, chapter 3—each time from a different point of view.

It is in this passage in the letter to the Philippians, more than in any other passage, that Paul tells us the inner effect on him of seeing the Lord Jesus on the road to Damascus. Looking at this passage (and also at a passage in the previous chapter) we shall see, first of all, what manner of man it was, according to his own words, who saw Jesus that day; then we shall see how afterwards he came to describe the true character of the vision he saw; and then the profound effect it had on him.

First, he describes himself as being full of pride, though at the time he was quite unaware of it. That is the usual thing with pride: you are quite unaware of it until the Holy Spirit shows you; then you see you are full of it. He begins by enumerating seven things which he had regarded as gains—seven things which he felt gave him status with men and with God. Even God, he thought, must have regard to a man with these things to his credit. These things can be reduced to four. The first was *pride of ancestry:* "Circumcised the eighth day, of the stock of Israel, of

the tribe of Benjamin, an Hebrew of the Hebrews."
Circumcision on the eighth day marked him out from
the rest of the nations, whom the Jews always re-
ferred to contemptuously as "the uncircumcised."
More than that, he says, he was of the stock of Israel;
that is, he was no Gentile proselyte, lately come to
the faith, but one born of God's chosen race—certainly a matter for pride. Then he gloried in the fact
he was of the tribe of Benjamin, the tribe that gave
Israel her first king. We would say of him today, he
came from the "top drawer." That was something
Paul regarded with real satisfaction. Then he says he
was an Hebrew of the Hebrews. Although his family
was of the Jews of the dispersion, they had not let slip
their customs, as had some, but had continued them
with the greatest strictness. That too was a matter of
gratification to him. And I am sure that in all sorts of
ways he betrayed the fact that he looked down on
those who were not of the same ilk as himself.

We too may have pride of ancestry, albeit unsus-
pected, in our hearts. Racial pride and class pride do
not die immediately in the life of a believer. A new
set of circumstances may bring out the fact that we
are despising, criticizing, even hating another, because he comes from a background other than our
own—and it can divide our fellowship. After World
War II in Europe, when Christians from different
countries met, there arose in their hearts quite unex-
pectedly reactions of aversion and bitterness toward
one another, and I remember occasions when the
Holy Spirit had to deal with this very definitely in us.

Then the second thing that characterized Saul of
Tarsus was *pride of orthodoxy,* as seen when he said of
himself, "touching the law, a Pharisee." We are in-
clined to regard the name of Pharisee usually to

imply a hypocrite. That was far from always the case. The Pharisees were basically the orthodox people of the day, those who believed the Scriptures and held firmly to the old doctrines. They were the strict people, who fulfilled every jot and tittle of the law of Moses and wanted everybody else to do the same. To be a Pharisee put a man right up there—in his own estimation at least—far above the Sadducees, who were the liberals of the day. As such they did not believe certain doctrines of the Scriptures, saying, "There is no resurrection, neither angel, nor spirit."[1] Someone has said, "That is why they were 'sad you see.' " But Paul was one of the Pharisees who confessed both, one of the strictest and most orthodox of them. I imagine it was a matter of great gratification to him to be able to class himself as one of that group. We too can be Pharisees, proud of our orthodoxy, proud that we are not liberals in our view of the Bible, but true to it in its entirety and ready to take issue with anyone who believes otherwise. It is, of course, right to "earnestly contend for the faith which was once delivered unto the saints";[2] but never that we should take pride in our orthodoxy and in effect make it part of our righteousness. Be assured, this does lurk in our hearts; don't deny it! I had to learn something about this years ago. I found myself working in an evangelistic enterprise with liberal theologians and I did not like it, and I got rather hot under the collar. The Holy Spirit ultimately convicted me and showed me that I was saying, "I thank Thee, O Lord, I am not as these liberals." He showed me that the gospel was not to give me special status above others but for my desperate need as a sinner;

1. Acts 23:8.
2. Jude 3.

and could I say that my need as a sinner was any less than that of the liberal? Indeed, my sins were worse, because they were done against greater light.

Then there was *pride of activity* in Saul, as revealed by his phrase, "concerning zeal, persecuting the church." So great was his zeal for the religion of his fathers that he was full of activity in persecuting the latest deviating sect, the infant church of the Nazarene. His zeal and activity along these lines was something of pride to him, and how great was his gratification when the Sanhedrin were only too ready to give him authorization to go to Damascus to hunt the Christians down there. "None better fitted than yourself to undertake this task for us," I imagine the letter from the Sanhedrin read. Did he often look at that letter on headed notepaper with pleasure and say to himself, "They are taking note of my zeal and my activity; they think I am an up-and-coming man!" Saul had always thought so too, and he was glad to have this view of himself corroborated by the Sanhedrin. The busy Christian worker can likewise be proud of his zeal and activity. When he gets invitations to go here or there in the Lord's service he takes pleasure in the fact that he has been noticed as an up-and-coming man. I confess it used to be a matter of great pride to me that as an evangelist my engagement book was full for at least a year ahead and I was being increasingly called upon. How much it means to us can be seen by how we feel when we are not called upon and when others are preferred before us. With so many of us Christians it is activity, activity, activity—and I suspect that in an unexpressed way it has become part of our righteousness.

Then the fourth and perhaps the worst thing that characterized him was *pride of morality*, as seen from his next words, "touching the righteousness which is in the law, blameless." He felt he had done all the law, kept all the rules and been as strict with himself as he knew how, and as a result could be regarded as blameless. And frankly, you and I would have found it difficult to fault him in the matter of his religious observance and moral performance as far as the outward eye could see. But the unpleasant thing about him was that it was he who said he was blameless, and quite obviously he got pleasure from it and felt it gave him superior status with men and put him right with God. Pride, always an unpleasant thing, becomes particularly odious when it expresses itself in the realm of morals and religion. This is the real heart of a Pharisee, and that heart is in all of us. Our inward thought so often is, if not in one matter then in another, "I thank Thee I am not as other men." We don't do this, we don't do the other; we don't miss our quiet times, we don't fail to give money, we don't dress in a worldly way, or go to worldly amusements. We little know how much these things mean to us until we find ourselves with people who do what we don't do and who don't even appear to be trying. Then we find ourselves looking down at them as from some pedestal of pride. How little we know what the law of God really demands of us! We seem to think that provided we keep certain rules it does not matter what happens in other areas. But those other areas where self is allowed to reign untouched are the important ones.

Now all these things had to do with Saul's righteousness, that is, his rightness with God. All his efforts were directed to adding to his store of righteousness. He wanted to excel his contemporaries in the Jewish religion and he succeeded, and was seen to succeed. He was indeed the man going up, getting better and better, more and more highly thought of. Like him we are men going up, or who desire to go up, and like him our great concern is with our righteousness. So many of our activities are directed to adding to our store of righteousness before God and before our fellows. We want to keep up with and excel, if possible, the other man in that realm. Let it be said clearly, we love our righteousness more than anything else, as seen by the fact that we are so loath to let it go and admit ourselves to be wrong. Speaking personally, I hate above all to admit I am wrong, and will argue and argue that I am right, which only shows how much I really love my righteousness. Job was like that. He was willing to lose his wealth, his children, his health, if God so decreed. But he was not willing to lose his right-eousness. He could not bear the accusation of his three friends who, trying to console him, said he must have done something wrong to account for his many troubles. Chapter after chapter he wearies us with saying "I am right, I am right. I will hold fast my integrity, I will not let it go." He loved his righteous-ness more than he loved his wealth, his family, or even his health. And so do we all, shown by the vehemence with which we argue we are right. Job was, indeed, a man going up, and he could not bear to come down.

This, then, is the manner of man, Saul of Tarsus, who met the Lord Jesus on the road to Damascus.

Now we come to what it was that was revealed to him when he had this vision. I want you to use a little imagination. Let us repeat the facts first. A light from heaven prostrates him; a supernatural Person speaks to him and charges him with persecuting Him, and when asked His name, says "I am Jesus, whom thou persecutest." Paul was astonished and might have said, "Jesus? this supernatural Person is Jesus? But that man was put to death on a cross with all the nation united against Him, thinking Him to be an impostor. What in the world does this mean?" He had three days in which to find out. For those days he was smitten with blindness and could do nothing but think and think, and as he did so he began to understand. "That supernatural Person was God; and since He stated He was Jesus, then the One we put to death on the cross was God. Then what He declared about Himself was right . . . and the rest of us were wrong. More than that, for Him to die as a Man on the cross meant that He had had to come down, a long way down, from so great a height, to so great a depth; and for whom did He do it, if it was not for me, Saul of Tarsus?"

If Saul was the man going up, Jesus was the Man coming down. And when the man going up met that other One coming down, it broke him; and what things were gain to him, he counted loss, and the Pharisee took his place as a sinner before God in a way he had never done before.

Years after, when his understanding and vision of Jesus had matured much more, he wrote down what it was he really perceived—it is contained in the same Epistle to the Philippians, but in the previous chapter, chapter 2.

This great passage describes the Man coming down and begins with the injunction that we are to let the mind (or disposition) be in us that was also in Christ Jesus. Then he describes that disposition, and we see it as the disposition that is ever willing to give up its rights and go down for others. I want you to look carefully at these verses[3] and at the grammar of them. They begin with "Jesus . . . being in the form of God." Can we imagine any higher status than was His, surrounded by the worship of heaven? There is only one direction He can go, if He is to move at all, and that is down.

Then we are told one thing He did not do with regard to His equality with God: "Who being in the form of God, He counted it not a prize to be on an equality with God" (I quote from the English Revised Version of 1881 here). A prize is something one is eager to grasp, and when one has it, unwilling to relinquish. To Jesus, equality with God was no prize, shown by the fact that when man's great need required it, He gladly let it go. How unlike us! We may be doing some piece of service and imagine it is done solely for the glory of God, but if we should be asked to relinquish it in favor perhaps of another, we are in a tumult and are unwilling to let it go. As the event shows, it was more of a prize to us than we ever thought. It was doubtless so with Saul of Tarsus— there were so many things which he counted prizes. But not so with Jesus; equality with God was no prize to Him.

Then the verses tell us two things He did do. First, "but emptied Himself." The Authorized Version here is beautiful, "He made Himself of no reputation"; but "emptied Himself" is the real meaning of the Greek. For us He gladly emptied Himself of His visible glory and said farewell to all that it meant. What a costly renunciation!

Then follows a clause which amplifies this act of self-emptying: "taking upon Him the form of a ser-

3. Phil. 2:5–8.

vant." The Greek word is not *diakonos*. the usual word for servant, but *doulos* which means "slave." The Revised Standard Version usually translates the word *doulos* as "slave" wherever it appears in the New Testament—and properly so. But here, strange to say, the translators chose to put the word "servant" in the text, with "slave" only in the margin as an alternative. Could it be they could not bear to put baldly that Jesus took upon Himself the position of a slave, so shocking is the thought; for a slave has no rights, no wages, no union, no right to strike. The position of a slave is something utterly unacceptable to our social structure today. But that is the position that Jesus took for us, that of one who has no rights. He let them tread on Him, do what they liked, and that without resistance on His part. Then follows a further complementary phrase: "being made in the likeness of men."[4] In all things He was made like unto His brethren. Forsaking His high status He stooped to be part of our humanity with all its weaknesses and pains. He did not say, "You become like Me," but rather, "I am come to be like you." Here we see, then, the Man coming down, God's self-emptied Servant. What an embarrassment, to say the least, to that other man going up!

But here is a second thing He did: having emptied Himself, "He humbled Himself." As if the stoop from Deity to humanity was not great enough, He went lower still, "and being found in fashion as a man, He humbled Himself."[5] Our conception of power is to humble others; God's is to humble Himself. Saul of Tarsus' word was "Exalt thyself "; the Son of God's word was "I humble Myself." This meant for Him not

4. ERV
5. ERV

only submitting to all sorts of indignities that Saul would never have tolerated, but humbling Himself in a much more important matter, as the next phrase shows: "becoming obedient unto death."[6] This was His supreme act of self-humbling. If God should require it, He was willing as an act of obedience even to give up His right to live; and God did require it, and He bowed His head. Thus it was He stooped not only from Deity to humanity, but also to mortality. With Charles Wesley we say with wonder:

> 'Tis mystery all! the Immortal dies:
>   Who can explore His strange design?
> In vain the first-born seraph tries
>   To sound the depths of love divine.

Surely, you say, that is the lowest point to which He can go! No, there is a second qualifying phrase which adds, "even the death of the cross." That is the lowest place of all, a place of utter disgrace. For you see, there are different sorts of deaths. There is death on a bed, or death on a field of battle. There is nothing necessarily disgraceful about such deaths. But Jesus did not die on a bed, nor on a field of battle, but on a cross; and the cross was a punishment reserved only for criminals. And as He died like that, out in the open for everyone to see, the crowd could not but infer that He was a criminal. As they saw it, only criminals died on crosses. There was a criminal on a cross on one side and a criminal on a cross on the other side, and it seemed obvious to them that He must be one too. They did "esteem Him stricken, smitten of God, and afflicted"[7] on His own account.

6. *ERV*
7. Isa. 53:4

And Jesus never disabused them. He never hasted to tell them that He was not a criminal at all, that He was dying for other people's sins. He did not do what Job did, refuse the unjust accusation and protest His innocence. He just let them think He was a criminal. In other words, He let go what is every man's most precious possession, His righteousness—that He might give it to us. He let go what Job would not let go, what Saul of Tarsus would not let go, and what you and I will not let go. In the deepest way possible He was content to be numbered with sinners, and classed as one Himself—and that was the bottom place, the final surrender of self.

That was what Saul of Tarsus saw, and it took him three days at least to see it. We can say, putting it another way, that he saw the brokenness of Deity. Brokenness is the opposite of hardness. Hardness says, "You are to blame"; brokenness says, "I am to be blamed." For long centuries God had sought to bring man to accept the blame that He might then freely forgive him and restore him. In the course of history God had sought to bring man to penitence by many and grievous disciplines, but all to no avail. Man had only stiffened his neck. And thus it was as if God said, "If man will not take the blame, there is only one thing left for Me to do—I must take the blame." And that is what God did in the Person of His Son on Calvary's cross: He took on Himself man's blame. And that was the brokenness and love of the Deity that this self-righteous Pharisee was made to look upon that day, and we too.

What was the effect that this vision had on Saul? Let him speak for himself: "What things were gain to me, those I counted loss for Christ. Yea doubtless, and I count all things but loss for the excellency of the knowledge of Christ Jesus, my Lord; for whom I have suffered the loss of all things and do count them but refuse."[8] Such was the love he looked upon that he did not know where to put himself, or how to hide his face. He was a broken man. The brokenness of the Deity provoked the brokenness of the creature, as it was designed it should. He counted but utter loss all those things he had previously regarded as gains, and so was prepared to take his true place, the sinner's place. Doing so, he cast away his own pathetic righteousness in order to embrace Christ as his own. It was as if he cried out to the One on the cross: "Thou art not the criminal, I am the criminal! At last I am willing to confess it and I come to Thee, the lover of all such." And he not only counted loss those things that used to be gains to him, but when he came actually to suffer the loss of them—to be dropped out of polite society and the circles of influence he had known and to be in actuality treated by the authorities as a criminal—he did not regret the loss of those things, but spoke of them as so much refuse compared to the infinitely better things he was now enjoying in Christ. The man going up was content to be the man going down with Jesus.

This is ever the effect upon us of a vision of the cross. It changes many things for us, but chiefly our attitude to our righteousness and our reputation, to the things that used to be gain to us. As long as we love our righteousness and are not prepared to lose our reputation, we sweep our sins under the carpet, for our pride forbids us to repent. But when we see Jesus losing His reputation, His all, for us, then we

8. Phil. 3:7–8.

are melted by the love of it and are willing to be broken and take a sinner's place. We are willing to be known as we really are, to turn back the carpet and allow Jesus to apply His blood that cleanses from all sin. It means that we count as nothing all those things we thought gave us status before God and man. To use a colloquialism, what price our racial background or social class, our spiritual orthodoxy, our zealous activity or our apparent morality? These things never saved us from sinning, and when we have sinned they do nothing to restore us to peace. We have to go out from them all, to count them but loss, in order to go to the cross with everybody else, there to be made whole by the blood of Jesus Christ. Not only does the cross restore us to God again, but it breaks down those middle walls of partition, those distinctions in which pride is entrenched, by making nothing of them.

A new vision of the cross, however, does more. It shows that God has set forth His Son last of all, and that by deliberate intent. He has so arranged it that there is no suffering, no indignity, no deprivation of rights, no injustice that men suffer that Jesus has not suffered Himself and that to a far greater degree. The effect is to shame us out of our complaints, self-pity, and resentment, and help us to bend our necks and surrender our wishes and rights to God, even as He did on the cross for us.

Missionaries brought back to England in 1947 from revival in East Africa a little chorus that summarized what they had been learning.

> Lord, bend that proud and stiff-necked I,
> Help me to bend the neck and die;

Beholding Him on Calvary,
Who bowed His head for me.

I cannot do better than to include here a short writing by the Rev. John Collinson on the subject of brokenness, which I reproduce here with his permission:

Sometimes it is asked what we mean by brokenness. Brokenness is not easy to define but can be clearly seen in the reactions of Jesus, especially as He approached the cross and in His crucifixion. I think it can be applied personally in this way:

When to do the will of God means that even my Christian brethren will not understand, and I remember that "neither did His brethren believe in Him,"[9] and I bow my head to obey and accept the misunderstanding, *this is brokenness.*

When I am misrepresented or deliberately misinterpreted, and I remember that Jesus was falsely accused but He "held His peace," and I bow my head to accept the accusation without trying to justify myself, *this is brokenness.*

When another is preferred before me and I am deliberately passed over, and I remember that they cried "Away with this man, and release unto us Barabbas,"[10] and I bow my head and accept rejection, *this is brokenness.*

When my plans are brushed aside and I see the work of years brought to ruins by the ambitions of others, and I remember that Jesus allowed them to "lead Him away to crucify Him"[11] and He accepted that place of failure, and I bow my head and accept the injustice without bitterness, *this is brokenness.*

9. John 7:5.   10. Luke 23:18.   11. Matt. 27:31.

When in order to be right with my God it is necessary to take the humbling path of confession and restitution, and I remember that Jesus "made Himself of no reputation" and "humbled Himself . . . unto death, even the death of the cross,"[12] and I bow my head and am ready to accept the shame of exposure, *this is brokenness.*

When others take unfair advantage of my being a Christian and treat my belongings as public property, and I remember "they stripped Him," and "parted His garments, casting lots,"[13] and I bow my head and accept "joyfully the spoiling of my goods" for His sake, *this is brokenness.*

When one acts towards me in an unforgivable way, and I remember that when He was crucified Jesus prayed "Father, forgive them; for they know not what they do,"[14] and I bow my head and accept any behavior towards me as permitted by my loving Father, *this is brokenness.*

When people expect the impossible of me and more than time or human strength can give, and I remember that Jesus said, "This is my body which is given for you . . . ;"[15] and I repent of my self-indulgence and lack of self-giving for others, *this is brokenness.*

Paul tells us that in making his surrender to Jesus he was not only motivated by the love of the cross, but by the sight of a whole set of better gains (there are *seven* of them) that would be his if he was prepared to discard the old ones (there were seven of *them* too). He tells us that he counted all things but loss for "the excellency of the knowledge of Christ Jesus, my Lord." Excellency simply means that which excels. In

12. Phil. 2:7, 8.
13. Matt. 27:28, 35.

14. Luke 23:34.
15. Luke 22:19.

other words, the knowledge of Christ Jesus utterly excelled in value what he was giving up.

What then were these new gains? First, "that I may win Christ." What a gain for Paul and for us! What does it matter if, in repenting, I have to lose my reputation, provided I find Jesus again? I find that when it comes to an issue, I cannot have my own righteousness and Jesus. If I am not prepared to lose my righteousness, I will miss Jesus. But what matters what else I lose, provided I have Him again?

But he gained something else: "I count all things but loss . . . that I may . . . be found in Him, not having mine own righteousness, which is of the law, but that which is through faith in Christ, the righteousness which is of God by faith."[16] This was a new and perfect righteousness before God, infinitely better than his own tattered one. And he got it when he counted all else but loss to take a sinner's place. In other words, when you and I are prepared to confess we are wrong, God says we are right, as right with Him as the blood of His Son can make us. He has waited long to see our pride broken and hear us confess on some point "O God, I am wrong." But the moment we do so, we are credited from the cross with a perfect righteousness before God, in which righteousness we may be as free as a bird in our relationship with Him. Of course, this imputed righteousness has been ours since the day of our conversion in an overall sense, but justification by faith is intended by God to be a contemporary, joyous experience, for lack of which the saints are dragging their feet and struggling on in their own strength, without peace and gladness. And the lack of this experience is due simply to the lack of broken-

16. Phil. 3:8–9 ERV.

ness and repentance at the cross of Jesus as oft as the Spirit convicts us.

We will just mention one more of his gains here.

"I count all things but loss . . . that I may know Him, and the power of His resurrection." Resurrection, like revival, simply means receiving life again. It presupposes there has been a dying, a going down, and tells us that where that is so there is intended to be a coming up again, a living again. Paul in effect says that he wants to know the coming up again of the Lord Jesus after he has gone down to the cross. There was a coming up again for Jesus; so there is for you and me. Paul wants to know how to come up in praise and faith after he has been brought low through adversity, sickness, opposition, or anything that Satan can bring. If he is made to bear about in his body the dying of Jesus Christ, he wants the life of Jesus to be manifested in his mortal body; rather like a cork—the deeper it is submerged, the more certainly it comes up. I am sure that he also meant that he wanted to come up in praise and faith after he had humbled himself in repentance, and he wants to know the power of it so that he comes up quickly and does not take a long time about it. He wants his coming up to be a real coming up where his chains fall off and his heart is free. For that, he says, he gladly counts all things but loss.

We are sometimes told by our teachers that we should not live the up-and-down life, and the saints cringe as they hear it because they know that is just the sort of life that is so often theirs. Be careful, you teachers, lest you put the saints under law and fail to show them the way of grace and gladness. It is, however, quite true that we ought not to be living the up-and-down life, but we *should* be living the down-

and-up life! Down to the cross in repentance and up again through the power of His blood in praise to God; down to give in on some new point on which we are convicted and then up again to praise Him for restoration and peace; down to surrender our rights on some matter and up again to have His life living anew in us. And not only in such matters as these are we to know the down-and-up life, but in every other circumstance or difficulty where we are brought low. Phillips translates Paul's phrase in 2 Corinthians 4:9, "cast down, but not destroyed," as "knocked down, but not knocked out." We come up again because we have in us the same life that was in Him.

This, then, was what happened to Saul of Tarsus when he saw the Lord. The man going up saw that other Man coming down, and it broke him and he joined Jesus on the way down, which he found, as Jesus did, was in reality the way up.

Job, like Paul, ended up as a broken man and like Paul found this the path into infinitely greater blessing, "twice as much as he had before" as the old account has it. He did not, of course, have a vision of the cross, as Paul did, but he certainly had an awesome vision of the Almighty, which caused him to humble himself to the dust. He could resist his friends when they spoke, but not when God Himself spoke to him and revealed Himself. Listen to what he says as a result: "I have heard of Thee by the hearing of the ear, but now mine eye seeth Thee. Wherefore I abhor myself, and repent in dust and ashes."[17] If you are a reader of the Authorized Version you will see that the word "myself" is in italics, meaning that it does not appear in the original Hebrew. The trans-

17. Job 42:5–6.

lators had to supply a word in order to make sense. The margin of the Revised Version of 1881 has put "my words" instead of "myself," so that the sentence reads "Wherefore I abhor my words and repent in dust and ashes." They've got it—that surely is the right word, for it is in accordance with the whole message of the book. What Job repented of was not the sins of which his friends accused him, for he had not done them; but his words. He said, "My words, my words! What have I been saying? God forgive me for my words of self-justification before man and Him." He cast aside his righteousness and took a sinner's place in the matter of the sin of self-justification if of no other, for in God's sight none is right. From that moment of brokenness everything for him changed—you can read for yourself the moving story of the grace God bestowed on him as a result. He too found the way down to be the way up.

Then . . . came Jesus and stood in the midst, and saith unto them, Peace be unto you. And when He had so said, He showed unto them His hands and His side. Then were the disciples glad, when they saw the Lord.

John 20:19–20

Now the God of peace, that brought again from the dead our Lord Jesus, that great Shepherd of the sheep, through the blood of the everlasting covenant, make you perfect in every good work to do His will, working in you that which is well-pleasing in His sight, through Jesus Christ, to whom be glory forever and ever. Amen.

Hebrews 13:20–21

But Christ being come an High Priest of good things to come, by a greater and more perfect tabernacle, not made with hands, that is to say, not of this building, neither by the blood of goats and calves, but by His own blood He entered in once into the Holy Place, having obtained eternal redemption for us.

Hebrews 9:11–12

4

WHEN THE DISCIPLES SAW HIM.

The Vision of the Blood.

"And when He had so said, He showed unto them His hands and His side. Then were the disciples glad, when they saw the Lord." Here is another result of seeing Jesus. Seeing Him risen from the dead and seeing His hands and His side, the sad were made glad. Such a change from sadness to gladness is a simple and wonderful thing, and it happens to us when we see Jesus risen from the dead and *that He was brought again from the dead through the blood of the everlasting covenant.* This is why I have linked on the opposite page the verse in John 20 with that in Hebrews 13. Speaking for myself, I have not always seen that Jesus was brought again from the dead through the blood of the everlasting covenant, as Hebrews 13 says, and I have not always found peace through the sight of Him like this, as I do now.

I believe this aspect of things is especially for those in a certain condition; for those who know they have not been living a victorious life, who mourn over their failures and repent of them, but who still feel condemned and do not feel glad in the Lord. Repentance, essential as it is, does not in itself give the guilty conscience peace, or take away its stain. Such people as have been described can still be taking a stick to themselves. These need the vision of the mighty power of the precious blood of Christ by which He Himself was brought again from the dead, and to see that the efficacy of that blood is for them too.

We must look together into this in greater detail. In Romans 4:25 Paul says that Jesus "was delivered for our offenses, and was raised again for our justification." There are two things here. Jesus "was delivered for our offenses," meaning He took responsibility for the sins of the world, the sins of the lost and the sins of the saints, their past sins and their future sins. As the old gospel song says,

> He took my sins and my sorrows,
> He made them His very own.

The moment He did this He was delivered for our offenses and that by God's decree. That was the justest thing that ever happened in the universe. Regarded only as the sinless Son of God, it was an act of gross injustice; but when the sinless Son of God became our Surety and took responsibility for our sins, it was just of God to deliver Him to the cross, because that is what our sins deserve. You might well have thought He would stay there forever; for if the wages of sin is death, how long is that death to last?

What is our surprise when we find God raising Him from the dead the third day!—for He "was raised again for our justification." How is it that God is able to raise Him from the dead if the wages of sin is death?

A little boy came out of Sunday School one day to be met by a kindly gentleman who asked him a few questions, gently teasing him. The little boy took it very seriously. "What have you been doing in there?" asked the man. "I've been learning about Jesus," said the boy. "And who is Jesus?" asked the man, "and what did He do and what happened to Him?" The little boy told him all he knew, finishing with the story of how wicked men had put Him to death on the cross. Then the little boy walked away. Very soon, however, he ran back and said breathlessly, "Please, sir, I didn't tell you everything; He didn't *stay* dead."

Now, why did He not stay dead? How can a holy God bring His Son again from the dead when He is bearing the sins of the whole world? This verse in Hebrews 13 tells us that it was by one way alone, "through the blood of the everlasting covenant." The value of His blood shed in death was enough for all the sins for which He took responsibility, because of the infinite value of the Person whose blood it was. Its value was greater than all the sin of man and it fully paid the price of it. That was the significance of His last great cry on the cross, "It is finished!" The grave, therefore, had no right to continue to hold Him, for in His judgment-bearing on the cross He had paid its awesome price.

> If Jesus had not paid the debt,
> He ne'er had been at freedom set.

But because He has been set at freedom, and that by
His blood, it means He is clear of all the sins for
which He took responsibility. Sin has lost its power
to condemn Him any longer. But the sins of which
He is clear are my sins. Therefore, if my Surety is
clear, I am clear too. If by His blood sin has lost its
power to condemn my Substitute, it has lost its
power to condemn me also. I can be as clear of sin as
my Surety is.

> He bore on the tree the sentence for me,
> And now both the Surety and sinner are free.

It may sound daring to say it, but it is true, that if His
blood was enough to bring Him from the dead, it is
certainly enough to bring me again out of all the
darkness and deadness that sin brings, for He had
more sins reckoned to Him than I ever had. The most
I could have would be my own; He had the world's.
So it is that if He lives, and that by His blood, I can
live too—and that by the same blood.

When a sad, despairing heart sees that, he is glad.
Till we see Jesus and the meaning of His blood we
will always be sad, mourning over our failures, and
ever struggling for a better righteousness before God
and never finding rest. Indeed, the more we try, the
more self-condemned we will be. But when by the
revelation of the Spirit we see Jesus risen from the
dead by His blood, and that He has finished the work
to put us right with God, we shall have joy indeed and
can rest from our futile struggles to put ourselves
right. We shall see that we cannot be more right with
God than what the blood of Jesus makes us when we
call sin, sin.

Yes, this way of peace does involve us in calling

sin, sin. It does imply repentance, but what I am trying to say is that repentance in itself is not enough. You can still be sad after having repented. By faith we must see Jesus and His blood. Then the sinner has peace, then he is set free from his struggles.

Isaiah 30:15 sets this out beautifully: "For thus saith the Lord God, the Holy One of Israel: in returning and rest shall ye be saved." There are two conditions here if God's salvation is to come to us in a new way. First, there is returning—which is simply repentance, returning to the Lord. And then, resting. For many of us, however, it is too often "in returning and *resolving*"—in repenting and making new promises. But that is to put us again on the ground of works in spite of having repented. But when we have seen the blood of Jesus we do not talk like that; it is in returning and *resting.* Now that we have returned we can take it that we are right with God by the power of the blood of Jesus; we can rest with regard to our righteousness before God. We can also rest with regard to all the consequences of our sin and folly. Once the man in the middle of the mess he has created has repented, he can rest with regard to that mess, for God not only forgives but delights to take over the situation that has been created and make a new thing out of it. As someone has said, "Jesus not only forgives the messer, but unmesses the mess." And so it is that the returning one can rest on that count too, and see the Lord do wondrous things for him.

The Epistle to the Hebrews not only tells us that He was brought again from the dead through the blood of the everlasting covenant, but also that He went back again into heaven, into the Holy of Holies of God's presence, by that same blood. "Neither by the blood of goats and calves, but by His own blood He entered in once into the Holy Place, having obtained eternal redemption for us." Not even He, once He had taken the sinner's place, could enter into the Holy Place except by the merits of His own blood. With this passage I always like to link Psalm 24: "Who shall ascend into the hill of the Lord? Or who shall stand in His Holy Place? He who hath clean hands, and a pure heart, who hath not lifted up his soul unto vanity, nor sworn deceitfully. He shall receive the blessing from the Lord, and righteousness from the God of his salvation." If those are the conditions, then I for one am barred; for my hands have not always been clean, nor my heart always pure. I have often lifted up my soul unto vanity and I have sworn deceitfully to my neighbor. Therefore I cannot ascend to the hill of the Lord, or stand in His Holy Place. I am in the position of a motorist who turns the corner to find that a pair of those railway barriers has just come down to bar his way. And so it is we are all excluded from that place of deepest fellowship with God. But later in the psalm I see those barriers lifted up as the King of Glory, the Man of Sorrows, approaches . . . coming with His own blood. I hear the words, "Lift up your heads, O ye gates; and be ye lifted up, ye everlasting doors; and the King of glory shall come in." Who is this King of glory? He is the One who bore the sinner's sins upon the cross. How does such a One go into the Holy Place again? He does so, not with the blood of goats and calves, as the high priest entered into the inner sanctuary in the days of old, but with His own blood. He does not go in merely because He is the Son, but because His own blood has cleared Him of all the sinner's sins and thus gives Him a perfect title to return to that Holy Place again. And if the blood was enough for Jesus, to bring *Him* into the Holiest, it is enough for *me* and *I* may enter in. He has gone into the Holy of Holies and has left the door open for me.

In another place the Epistle to the Hebrews tells us He has gone in as our forerunner: "where the forerunner is for us entered."[1] And where the forerunner goes, others follow later. It was as if Jesus said, "Father, I have come back from the battle of Calvary, but I am only the forerunner—there is a great crowd coming along behind." And what a crowd it is, all of them maimed and crippled by their own sins, mighty sinners, but each one of them saved by mightier grace. They are coming in by the same way in which their forerunner came, by the mighty power of the blood of Jesus. Dare to believe in it and enter into the Holiest too.

If you are still mourning and blaming yourself it is not because God is blaming you; He has put the blame on Jesus. It can only be due to one of two things. Either that you have not really repented, or, more likely, you are mourning over your lost righteousness. Perhaps you feel that, having been saved for so long, you should not be failing as you are, that surely by now your wings should have grown! But your recent failures show that they have not grown at all and you are in effect saying, "Alas for my lost righteousness." That is nothing but pride. Accept the fact that you are a sinner and praise God that the blood of Jesus is your righteousness and that you have Him as your heavenly High Priest, who is there for you, showing His side and spreading His

1. Heb. 6:20 ▸

hands. That is enough for God; it should be enough for you. Then when by faith you have this vision of Him, like the disciples of old you will be glad indeed and no more sad.

All this is an essential part of the victorious life.

It seems right here to share some thoughts as to what the victorious life really is in the light of this message of grace. One almost hesitates to mention the phrase "the victorious life," for some emphases on the subject have been at bottom so much of law that they have almost been the death of us as we have tried in vain to make them work.

As I see it, there are three aspects to what may be called the victorious life.

First, and most basic, there is *His victory over me.* Years ago, while in Brazil with a colleague, I heard a young theological student give his testimony as to what he had learned in the meetings we had been conducting, and he put things far clearer than we ever had done. After telling of his struggles for victory in his life and of his disappointment that an outstanding experience of the presence of God during a time of prayer had failed to give him victory, he said, "I have now come to see that the victorious life is not me conquering sin, but Him conquering me and breaking me each time that sin comes in, and taking me to the cross." Do you get it—not me conquering sin, but Him conquering me. What a victory it is when He prevails on us to break, to admit to sin and, where called upon by God, to be in the light with another about it! All our pride is against such action and sometimes, as in Jacob's case, there wrestles a Man with us till the dawning of the day until He succeeds in breaking us.

A group of us were sitting on the grass at a conference camp one day, having a time of fellowship. Some were missionaries and Christian leaders. As we shared together, first one and then another would admit to the fact that God had shown him some wrong attitude, some act of unlove in his work for the Lord, and that he had been helped to bring it to the cross. On each occasion, all the group would burst into a song praising the Lamb. As I walked away from the gathering (which was still continuing) I heard in the distance again and again the same burst of singing, and I said to myself, "There is another victory for Jesus . . . and another." Some of those testimonies were costly ones and involved a real obedience unto death, a dying to self, and only Jesus could have achieved that victory over them.

Then there is *His victory for me,* in setting me free from the hangover of guilt and self-accusation. What I mean is best understood by an illustration. A team of us were meeting and praying together when one of the group, a full-time Christian worker, indicated that he had something costly to share, something he felt he ought to tell us if we were to know him as he really was. He told us how some few years before there had been a grievous moral failure in his life. He had confessed it to God and to his superior in the work, who had agreed to allow him nonetheless to continue in his position. For a moment there was a stunned silence and then, one by one, we took our place as sinners beside him, confessing that though we might not have done what he had done in act, the thought and desire had more than once been in our hearts, which in God's sight was the same as the act. For myself, I thought it was a wonderful victory that he had been able to share it with us. But one of the others in commenting on this afterwards said of him, "I think he still needs to get the victory." What did he mean by that? Did he mean that he still needed to get to a place where he was never likely to do this thing again? We all knew that it was almost inconceivable that he would repeat such a thing. What he meant was that this brother was not yet glad, that he was still mourning over how he would appear in our eyes, and sorry for his lost righteousness. He had not yet got through the sense of shame to a place of praise to God for His complete redemption from it. This is our place so often over smaller or larger matters. This means we yet need to see the blood of Jesus and to accept by faith the new righteousness, the sinner's righteousness. True, we have lost the good Christian's righteousness, but we may yet again newly experience the sinner's righteousness—and there really never was any other available. When we accept that, then our testimonies, though they may be sometimes costly, will be mingled with many praises and given with gladness. And that is victory! This is the victory that Charles Wesley celebrates in his famous hymn:

> My chains fell off, my heart was free,
> I rose, went forth, and followed Thee.

He is not celebrating the attainment by the saint of some higher ground of sanctification, but the victory over guilt, self-recrimination, and sadness—which the most sinful of us may have when we see the blood of Jesus again. I believe we do ourselves great damage when we read into some of our hymns of testimony anything more than the sinner's testimony, and when we think to apply them to some attainment of sanctification rather than to a new experience of God's justification of the sinner. This, then, is the aspect of victory dealt with chiefly in this chapter; and this, along with the first aspect, is basic.

The third aspect of the victorious life is *His victory in me;* that is, Jesus Christ living His life again in me. As someone has said, there is only one victorious life and that is the life of the victorious Christ. It is illustrated by the Lord's parable of the Vine and the branches. We naturally begin by making the mistake of trying to be the vine ourself, by doing our best to produce those fruits which we imagine a Christian ought to produce. We fail utterly, because "in me (that is, in my flesh) dwelleth no good thing."[2] But Christ is the Vine, not us, and we but His branches. When, weary of our attempts to be a good vine, we take our place as branches and begin to abide (or dwell) in Him, He promises to abide (or dwell) in us. And what can be more victorious than Jesus dwelling in us? That which is produced is now not characteristic of the branch but of the Vine, who dwells in the branch by the sap, that is, by the Holy Spirit.

This aspect of the victorious life, however, is based on the first two aspects. Only as we are willing for Him to be breaking us and bringing us to the cross, and only as we are finding peace as sinners through His blood, does He give to us through His life within what we confess we otherwise lack so completely.

2. Rom. 7:18.

And it came to pass, when Joshua was by Jericho, that he lifted up his eyes and looked and, behold, there stood a man over against him with his sword drawn in his hand; and Joshua went unto him, and said unto him, Art thou for us, or for our adversaries? And He said, Nay, but as Captain of the host of the Lord am I now come. And Joshua fell on his face to the earth, and did worship, and said unto Him, What saith my lord unto His servant? And the Captain of the Lord's host said unto Joshua, Loose thy shoe from off thy foot; for the place whereon thou standest is holy. And Joshua did so.

Now Jericho was securely shut up because of the children of Israel: none went out, and none came in. And the Lord said unto Joshua, See, I have given into thine hand Jericho, and its king, and the mighty men of valor. And ye shall compass the city, all ye men of war, and go round about the city once. Thus shalt thou do six days.

Joshua 5:13—6:3

5

WHEN JOSHUA SAW HIM.

The Vision of the Captain.

We come now to the vision that Joshua had of the Lord before the battle of Jericho, and to the effect that it had on him and, indeed, on the whole campaign in which he was engaged.

There seems to be a progression in this series of visions we are considering, each one of them of increasing importance. We all need the vision that Isaiah saw of the Lord high and lifted up, and that which Saul of Tarsus saw on the road to Damascus, and that which the disciples saw on the resurrection evening. But we most certainly need the vision that Joshua saw before Jericho; the canvas would not be complete without it, and such a vision could be quite crucial for us.

Let me briefly recount the facts. The forty years in which the children of Israel had wandered in the wilderness had drawn to a close. The old unbelieving generation had died off and those of the new generation under Joshua were ready to be led into the Promised Land. There were two obstacles in their way. The first was Jordan, but that had been surmounted in a wonderful way by the miraculous power of God—and in the crossing of the river God had set His seal on Joshua's leadership. Now came the next obstacle, the fortified city of Jericho. It stood right in their way; they could never go further until it was overcome. But Joshua did not know how to overcome it, or what strategy to use. One day, as the sun was setting, Joshua went to walk in a field to think—and above all to worry. He felt very much the captain that day and was burdened with the weight of responsibility. More than that, he felt that the resources that were at his command were quite inadequate against the forces of such a city with its walls frowning down upon him. It would not have done for us to have said to him, "But Joshua, the Lord has brought you-already through Jordan." "I know it, I know it," he would have replied, biting his nails, "but this isn't Jordan, this is Jericho!"

Then suddenly he lifted up his eyes to see a man in front of him, with a strange and glorious appearance. He was apparently a man of war for a drawn sword was in his hand. Joshua immediately jumped to the ready, for he did not know if he was friend or foe. He went to him and said, "Art thou for us or for our adversaries?" or in other words, "Are you on our side or theirs?" The answer was "Nay," which means, neither; "but as Captain of the host of the Lord am I now come." In other words, He said "I am not on your side, neither am I on their side; you are on My side. I am Captain, not you." And not merely Captain, but "Captain of the host of the Lord." These words show that He was Captain not only of Joshua's army but of the infinite hosts of the Lord, and back of Him were unbelievable resources. Then He went on to say, "Loose thy shoe from off thy foot; for the place whereon thou standest is holy." In those words He claimed Deity for Himself.

Who then was this Person that appeared thus to Joshua with this great heart-subduing message? In the Old Testament there are certain strange appearances of a supernatural Person and Bible students are agreed that they are appearances of the eternal Son of God, even before His incarnation, and call them Christophanes. We can take it, therefore, that this was the Son Himself who appeared to Joshua—our Immanuel, the same One who desires to reveal Himself to us today when we are in the same state of need as Joshua was.

Indeed, we are often in that same state of need. Our way is barred ahead sometimes by various Jerichos. There are servants of God, called to His work and deeply involved in it, before whom there stands some fortified city which bars their progress. What it is will vary from Christian worker to Christian worker—problems, unresponsive hearts, dissension among the saints, opposition from the world, or just the frustration of the unfulfilled need for outreach in the work. Or these Jerichos may be in our family life—deep problems of relationships there, or loved ones who still withstand the Lord; or more personal still, inner inadequacies and failures in our own lives that block our progress. In such situations we feel ourselves, as Joshua did, very much captain. Who is going to tackle this situation if we don't? And the responsibility lies heavy upon us. But how? The resources at our command, our own wit and strength, seem woefully inadequate. The memory of the past interventions of the Lord are dismissed with the words, "But this situation is different." And so we struggle and worry and plan, defeated in actuality before we ever begin.

In such situations Jesus, just because He is what He is, wants to appear to us. But the great question is, in what capacity does He want to appear? Is He going to be for me, or for my adversaries? Is He going to "read me a lecture," telling me I am no good and discouraging me, and thus be my adversary; or am I going to find Him on my side? The latter is just about the most we can conceive, that we will find Him perhaps on our side, helping us to face our responsibilities in a better way. But the eternal Son of God wants to appear to us quite other. He would say to us that while He is certainly no adversary to us, He is not on *our* side—we are on *His* side. He has come as *Captain,* to take back the position we have usurped. He has no intention of helping us to be better captains, but to take over from us. More than that, He is Captain of the hosts of the Lord: He has infinite resources with which to implement His own designs—when we let Him be Captain. When that is so, the fact that we are so inadequate in the face of our Jerichos is neither here nor there; the battle is now to be His. If this is our Jesus, how absolutely wonderful; don't you feel like hugging His feet?

I want to look at the message from the Man with the drawn sword in greater detail and to do so from the negative point of view in order to highlight the positive. His message began with "Nay" and that is a

negative. The Lord has to say a big "Nay" to so much
in us if His positive plans are to be implemented.

I see three glorious negatives here. The word
"Nay" meant first that the taking of Jericho was not
Joshua's idea, but the Lord's. Joshua was thinking and
acting as if it was his idea. It was nothing of the sort; it
had been the Lord's idea from the very start. Joshua
needed this big "Nay" pronounced upon him. But
having received it, could there have been anything
more encouraging to him? He might well have said,
"The joy of it, it is His idea!"

Then there was a second negative. It was that this
city was not going to be taken by the strength of
Joshua's army, nor was it to be done by Joshua's
efforts. Said the Man with the sword drawn, "I am
Captain of the hosts of the Lord, and this city is going
to be taken, not by your army, but by My infinite
invisible one and in My own way." What a rest this
second negative brought to Joshua. He saw that if he
had had a huge army it would not have helped; the
fact that it was not as large as he would have liked was
therefore going to be no hindrance. Another Captain
and another army had taken the field. Joshua's army
was but a little section of it, and he himself but a
section leader.

I consulted my concordance at this point in my
preparation and I made a new discovery. I knew that
throughout the Old Testament one of the oft-
repeated titles of God was "the Lord of hosts"—or as
the French Bible puts it, "L'Eternel des armées." I
wanted to find out where the title first appeared. I
discovered that there was no appearance of it in the
Bible before this incident. One can only infer that
this great title of Deity took its rise from this revela-

tion of Himself to Joshua and that it was indeed an altogether new one. If Exodus 6:3 is a new revelation of God under the name of "Jehovah," then Joshua 5:14 is a new revelation of Jehovah under the name of "Jehovah of hosts." If the first is a revelation of the grace of God (for Jehovah is ever the name of grace), then the second is a revelation of the mighty power of that grace. It is a wonderful thing to know that we are the objects of the grace of God, but even more wonderful to know that back of it are all the armies of heaven with which to implement the designs of that grace. This endows the passage we are studying with a special importance, does it not?

And now back to the third negative. That word "Nay" also implied that this which was to be done was not for Joshua's glory but for the Lord's. That is why the method to be used was a ludicrous one to human eyes. Marching round the city seven days and then shouting was no way to take a city like Jericho. It was done in this feeble way to demonstrate that when the walls fell down and the city became defenseless, God was the doer of it and all the glory was due Him. That is the reason why God told Joshua that everything in the city was to be devoted to the Lord—some things to be devoted to destruction by fire, and other things brought into the treasury of the Lord. The people were to get nothing out of it; God was to have all the glory.

Here we have God's "Nay" pronounced on the three forms of our self-life which we have already considered and which we know intrude so easily.

First, the Lord says it is not going to be by *self-will*. The taking of your Jericho is not your idea, it does not originate with you. You say, "I must conquer

Jericho." Is that your idea? It is not, it is God's. He has already planned that it shall fall to us.

Years ago I remember a missionary telling me how revival came to his field in South Africa. Its real beginning was when a group of missionaries talked together on a veranda of a certain bungalow. For long they had been praying earnestly that God would revive their churches, the spiritual life of which had fallen into a sorry state; but nothing had happened. They had come together for a conference and had invited as a speaker one who was visiting the country from abroad, one who had himself met the Lord in the Welsh revival and who had had experience of the deeper workings of God. After one of the sessions they were talking together with him on the veranda. As they did so, their hearts became strangely warmed. It was Jesus drawing near to them as the Man with the drawn sword, the Captain of the hosts of the Lord. It was as if He said, "The revival of the church is not your idea; it is Mine and has been even before you prayed. I am come to implement My own plans." The missionary concerned told me that he could not describe what happened in that moment, except to say that each one of them had the absolute assurance that the thing that they had so long been pleading for was His will and plan to do right there. Thereupon they gave up trying to conquer His reluctance (for that is what they saw they had been doing in the way they had been praying) and simply began to lay hold of His willingness. In the weeks that followed God visited each of their needy churches with revival. The simple truth is that when Jesus is allowed to be Captain in a situation, the victory is never in doubt, not for a moment. His plans for every one of us are good plans, unbelievable plans, not dependent on our power or lack of it. This thing begins with Jesus and He is going to implement His own plans with His own power.

Then this negative implies a ban on our *self-effort.* That which He plans is not going to be implemented by *our* strength, or good qualities, but by the Captain of the hosts of the Lord. Our strong points are going to be no help, our weak ones no hindrance; it is going to be done in another way, by another One altogether—by His Spirit. "Not by might, nor by power, but by My Spirit, saith the Lord of hosts."[1]

I think this brings us to the third negative implied in this word "Nay." What is going to be done is not for *self-glory.* What He plans for you is not to be regarded as a prize for you, merely for your own gratification and glory, but supremely a prize, a blessing, for others through you, that He might be glorified in their eyes. We must judge as sin all other motives that come into our hearts. This is where Israel failed. Achan took for himself the spoil that was meant for God and victory ceased that moment until it was put right. I heard the story of a certain Welsh preacher whom God was using in the days of the revival in Wales. The one who told the story was accompanying him as he returned late at night after a meeting where the Spirit of God had done mighty things in people's lives. The preacher was strangely silent as they made their way through the darkness. Then suddenly he lifted up his voice and in tones that made the hills ring called out, "O God, You could do so much if You could trust us not to take the glory!"

1. Zech. 4:6 •

And now lastly, and most important, we come to the response of Joshua to this vision of the Lord, the effect that it had on him. "When I saw Him . . . ," what? "And Joshua fell on his face to the earth, and did worship." This was the most crucial moment in the whole campaign in which Israel was engaged, when their leader prostrated himself before the Captain of the hosts of the Lord. Before the walls of Jericho could fall, Joshua had to fall. In doing so, he vacated his own place and surrendered completely to the captaincy of the Captain of *the hosts of the Lord,* confessing the sin and folly of trying to be captain himself. That this falling on his face and worshiping was far more than a physical act is shown by the words immediately following, "What saith my lord unto His servant?" Those are the words of a subordinate to a superior. Joshua was willing for this new Captain to make the decisions and give the orders.

When we see Jesus as Captain of the hosts of the Lord, ours it is also to fall on our faces before Him and worship—that is, to confess the self-will, self-effort, and self-glory that have dominated us and deeply surrender to Him as the Captain, and be willing for Him to make the decisions, give the orders, and be the doer of the work. This is ever the turning point in our lives and in the enterprises we are engaged upon. We cannot be too low at His feet if He is to cause the walls of our Jericho to fall. He will have no difficulty with those walls if He can get us to fall first. There is no alternative; we must repent our way to that blessed low position at His feet, seeing first one thing and then another thing of self which has intruded to exclude Him from His true place. If self intrudes in attitudes a hundred times a day, we must judge it as sin a hundred times a day in order to

maintain this place at His feet, if He is to do miracles.
And if we find ourselves complaining that we do not
immediately see those miracles, that is another thing
of self to confess—because faith knows He is now in
control and will not fail.

> Lower and lower, down at Thy Cross,
>   All the world's treasure counting but dross;
> Down at Thy feet, blessed Saviour we fall,
>   Lower, still lower, Christ all in all.*
>
> —E. E. Hewitt

Then when Joshua said "What saith my lord unto
His servant?" the Lord began to talk to him. He
began by saying, "See, I have given into thine hand
Jericho, and its king, and the mighty men of valor."
Not "I will give it," but " I have given it to you
already." When Jesus is for us the Captain of the
hosts of the Lord, He tells us that the victory is ours
before we ever begin. We must believe this and take
up a corresponding attitude of faith and act accord-
ingly. Victory is not something in our outward activities, but rather something in our spirit before
those outward activities ever begin. "This is the victory that overcometh the world, even our faith," says
John in his first epistle. Faith is an attitude of heart,
and that attitude, we are told, is victory, even before
the battle begins. Some people are defeated before
they ever start. But others are victorious before they
have struck a blow! When He is the Captain of the
situation, He speaks so positively to us about everything that we must take up a corresponding attitude
of faith.

*From *Keswick Hymn Book.* Used by kind permission.

A falling on his face before the Captain of the host and an attitude of positive faith in Jehovah were the two effects of this vision on Joshua.

Then the Lord told Joshua the simple co-operation that he was to give to God—just walk around the walls once a day for six days and on the seventh day seven times and then, all together, one big shout! In doing this Joshua was not trying to do God's work for Him, as he would have done before. Had he been doing it, he would certainly have chosen some other method than those crazy actions. Such things were not calculated on the human level to produce any great results. But it was the necessary co-operation with Himself that God required of him.

Here we come to consider the distinction between us trying to do God's work for Him by our own efforts and schemes, and a right co-operation with Him. Make no mistake, we are certainly called to co-operate with Him, sometimes in the most active and strenuous ways. "Workers together with God" is one of the New Testament descriptions of believers. Where then is the distinction between striving in self-effort, and a right co-operation with God? It is a fine line where one begins and the other ends. Sometimes the very action which we had previously seen to be done in the flesh, we are clearly called of God on another occasion to do, but this time as an act of co-operation with Him.

There are actions, as this one with Joshua, where it is not likely to be one done in the flesh, because the thing we are called upon to do is so little calculated to produce a result, judged by human standards. On the other hand, there are cases where the things we are called to do by God are clearly calculated to produce exactly the result desired, as in the case of the strategy Gideon was told to use to put the Midianites to flight. He was told to surround the camp at night with his small band, each of whom was provided with a lighted torch inside an earthenware pitcher. At a given signal they were all together to break the pitchers, hold their torches high, and shout with one voice from all quarters, "The sword of the Lord and of Gideon!" The Midianites woke up in the middle of the night, and thinking they were surrounded by an army much greater than themselves, promptly fled with Israel in pursuit. The method used was calculated, even on a human level, to produce that result. Gideon might have said, "What a good idea! Why didn't I think of it myself? How original of God!"

Yes, when the Captain of the hosts of the Lord is on the field He is original in what He tells us to do and it is all so obviously effective too. But woe be to Gideon or to us if we say, "That was a good idea; I will try it again." The next time it may well be something that emanates purely from ourselves and is no real co-operation with God at all, and the result will invariably be nil.

Yes, it is a fine line and no one can give another any rules by which to judge. Each man himself must learn from the Lord, and he often has to learn by mistakes.

But turning more directly to the story before us, there are further lessons of co-operation with God for us to learn. There are two further things they were told to do. At the given moment Joshua told them, "Shout; for the Lord hath given you the city." This shouting was to be done while the walls were still standing, solely on the ground of faith. Against hope they were to believe in hope, being fully persuaded that what God had promised He was able also to perform, and they were to shout, that is, praise Him as if the walls had already fallen. This is the shout of faith to which God always delights to respond. This gift of faith was very much given to a friend of mine, with whom I used to work sometimes in evangelistic work. He used to pray in the most extraordinary way. I would sometimes hear him pray, "Lord, we thank Thee for the souls Thou hast saved tomorrow!" And when the meeting came the next day, God did just that, according to the faith we had expressed beforehand. This, of course, is the way which Jesus taught us to pray, though we may not always come up to it. "All things whatsoever ye pray and ask for, believe ye have received them, and ye shall have them."[2]

The other thing they were told to do was "Keep yourselves from the accursed thing."[3] They were to destroy, as to the Lord, what had to be destroyed—every bit of it—and to give to God what had to be given to Him. This is the place where failure came in. Achan took for himself certain things that should have been destroyed and other things that should have been given to God. And the victory ceased right there till it was put right. Great victories have certain perils for us, for in the hour of great blessing we may do what Achan did. We may spare what should be utterly renounced, or steal for ourselves glory that properly belongs only to God; and the results can be disastrous. Thank God, this can be put right at the cross of Jesus, who loves to restore what sin has deprived us of.

2. Mark 11:24 *ERV*.
3. Josh. 6:18.

I am a man of unclean lips, and I dwell in the midst of a people of unclean lips.

Isaiah 6:5

6

WHAT IS YOUR VISION?

The Vision of Revival.

As several friends of mine were discussing the theme that occupies these chapters, one of them said, "And shouldn't we say something on the subject, Have we a vision for Switzerland?" We were at the time taking part in a Bible Conference in Switzerland and it was natural that the name of that country should be the one that slipped out of his mouth. But what we all understood him to mean was, Had we each of us a vision for his own country? And if so what was it?

We are not now thinking about having a new vision of the Lord (we have considered that), but rather about having a vision for others. If we have had a vision of the Lord ourselves which has meant a new experience of revival in our lives, it is natural, surely, for us to have a vision of revival for others. This certainly seems to have been the case with Isaiah. We have already suggested that before he saw the Lord high and lifted up (in his chapter six) he was a man working without vision—without a vision of the Lord and without a vision for others. But when he got that new vision of the Lord he got a new vision for his people, and because of that God sent him to them. And although it involved many penetrating challenges to them, what a gloriously positive vision in the ultimate it was!

To have a new vision of revival for your whole country is perhaps more than you can rise to at first. Start nearer home—with your own home. Have you a vision of revival for your loved ones there and your relationship with them? Then have you a vision of revival for your fellowship group, and then for your church, and then for your country? We must not stop short of that. And if we have any such vision, what is the nature of it?

Years ago, soon after revival touched my own life, I went with Dr. Joe Church and William Nagenda* as a team to the Scripture Union center in Guebwiller, France, for a conference. After the meetings were over, William Nagenda took me quietly aside and asked me a simple question: "What is your vision?" And he waited for me to tell him what my vision was. I had been many years in the Lord's service as an evangelist before revival touched my heart, but my answer betrayed the fact that I had not understood what a true vision was. I said, "I suppose I have got three visions. For years I have been an evangelist, and I have this vision for evangelism still. And now I am working in a society that is occupied with the dis-

*These men were for many years two of the leaders in revival in East Africa.

tribution of the Scriptures and I have a vision for that line of things too. Also, in view of this new experience that has become mine, I have a vision for revival." He was deeply troubled over my answer, almost in despair over me. "Brother," he said, "you have not really seen the way yet. A vision for evangelism, a vision for Scripture, and a vision for revival—how terrible! There is only one vision, and that is Jesus, the Jesus you have been experiencing in revival; He includes everything."

Isaiah, in the chapter we have already considered, tells us how he got a vision for others. He tells us that in the light of that vision of the Lord he saw two things: first, "I am a man of unclean lips," and then, "and I dwell in the midst of a people of unclean lips." When he saw the Lord that day he not only saw himself as he really was but he saw the others around him as they really were, and he got a vision for them.

Let us remind ourselves about what he saw with regard to himself. In referring to his lips, we saw that he was referring to his service, for as a preacher his lips represented his service. And in saying that his lips were unclean, he meant to indicate that his service was unclean in God's sight; it was service done in the flesh, and as such it was utterly unacceptable in God's sight, nothing more than filthy rags. He never knew it until that day. And then came the live coal, and a new chapter in his life and service began.

He saw, too, that the same thing was true of everybody else around him; they all had the same problem. Not only was he a man of unclean lips, but he dwelt among a people of unclean lips. They were in exactly the same state of need as he was. He differed from them in only one thing: he knew now that his lips were unclean, but they didn't. They did not know that they were working in the flesh; they did not know that all their service was just filthy rags in God's sight. And more than that, they did not know that they didn't know—a double blindness. And so he got a vision and a burden for them.

A vision of revival for others begins, of course, with an experience of revival ourselves. That comes through seeing ourselves as we really are in the light of the holiness of God: that our best efforts are as unclean as our worst failures—that our service has been too often "of us, through us, and for us," and thus utterly unacceptable to God. It means a new experience of repentance and of the power of the blood of Jesus Christ to cleanse and restore; a new falling down at the feet of the Captain of the hosts of the Lord, for Him not merely to help us but for Him to take over. In short, it is a new experience of being filled with the Holy Spirit—for only through the Spirit does all this come about—and it is all based on seeing ourselves as we really are. By this experience we have passed from the place of uncertain searching for the answer, to complete assurance that we have found it in the Lord Jesus. No longer are we like Naaman when he said, "Behold, I thought, he will surely come out to me . . . and strike his hand over the place . . . and cure the leprosy," but we are like him when after being healed he said, "Now I know that there is no God in all the earth, but in Israel."[1] We have passed from "Behold I thought" to "Now I know." No longer are we looking for the answer for the Christian life in this direction, or that—along the lines of this emphasis, or that. "Now I know" is our testimony; the answer has been incarnated in our own experience.

1. 2 Kings 5:11, 15.

However, in seeing ourselves as we really are, our eyes have been opened to see others as they really are. Not only do we see that we are men of unclean lips, but we see that we dwell among a people of unclean lips—everybody else is in the same condition as ourselves. They too are working in the power of the self-life, their service too is but consecrated flesh and therefore utterly grieving to God. The only difference between us and them is that we know that our lips are unclean, but they don't know that theirs are. More than that, they don't know that they don't know—and go on in this double blindness, blissfully thinking all is well, doing their pathetic best as we had been doing. And as we see their need and their blindness to their need, we get a vision for them.

There need be nothing proud or critical in our saying what Isaiah did about those among whom we dwell. What is it that we have that others may not have? Our discovery is simply that we are bigger sinners than we thought we were and that Jesus is a bigger Saviour than we thought He was—no cause for pride in that, surely. Let us not fear, then, to see the need and blindness of those around us, for we shall not otherwise get the Lord's vision for them. Our vision for them is, first, that they might know that they don't know, that they might begin to realize there is something lacking; then, that they might see the hidden things about themselves that God would have them see; and then, that they may know Jesus coming to them to cleanse them from their sin and take over, as symbolized in the live coal.

Do not fear, then, to look around you with complete realism in the light of what you have seen in yourself. Your fellowship group, your church, your minister, the other churches throughout the land

and, closer at hand, the dear ones in your own family—everywhere you look people are going on in this double blindness, not knowing, and not knowing that they don't know. And then get God's loving vision for them, that He wants to open their eyes and bring them to a new reality and liberty.

You may say, What should I actually do about revival in this or that area around me? I believe the answer is, Don't do anything yet; just get from God a vision for them. God seldom does anything without first giving somebody a vision for it. Although you may feel there is hardly anything you can do for revival here or there, first get a vision for it. Be one of those who sigh for the desolations of Jerusalem.

Such a vision will obviously lead to prayer for various ones, and as you pray you will enter into the pain of God's heart over them. Then such prayer will doubtless lead you to give them your testimony as to what God has done in your heart, as one person to another, or to some group that gathers. God uses our personal sharing, more than anything else, to bring revival blessing to other lives.

Above all, I suggest you pray that God will give you a team for revival, with whom you can stand on the same ground at the cross. And start asking for, and looking for, just one person. Some people torment themselves because they have the picture of a whole church or mission station being revived at once and all together—and it never happens. Be content for God to begin with just one and to give that one to you. He or she may well be the one who gets helped through hearing what God has done in your life. Love will bind you together. Or it may be the one to whom you have had to go in real brokenness in order to be reconciled with him. If you look to God for but one He may well give you more than one, and then add others—and you can pray together as a team for this one and that one and act with God together.

I remember my first visit to the United States years ago, when four of us went together as a team to bring to that great country this simple message of grace and revival. I remember my brother Dr. Joe Church praying one prayer again and again: "O God, give us just one man. If You give us just one man in America who has seen Jesus and known deeper brokenness at His cross, then we can go home and say 'Revival has come to America.'" It was so restful—we were not looking for big crowds; it did not matter whether there were few people or many; we had come to America for only one man. God gave us, as you can well imagine, more than one man. But one man would have been enough, one man who would be, as a result, a team with us, even across the ocean.

Here let me go more deeply into what it means to be a team for revival. It begins with just one man who knows that he knows. He has passed from "Behold I thought" to "Now I know." And then there is another man who knows, and knows that he knows. But they are not yet a team, not yet in deepest fellowship for revival. That does not begin to take place until there has been a deep sharing between them and the first man knows that the second man knows; and when, as a further step, the second man knows the first man knows that he knows. Then the two of them know they are in something precious together and can share their concerns for God's working in other lives and can pray and move together to that end.

I remember this is how God brought to birth His team for revival in England back in 1947, which team has continued and increased to this day. As a result of those who came back from East Africa to share with us what they had been learning in revival, a number of leaders were deeply blessed and helped. To begin with we hardly knew one another at all, only we heard that this one and that one had been giving a new sort of testimony to the people in his church. One of them invited some ten of us to spend two days together in his vicarage. We spent those days sharing deeply with one another what Jesus had been doing in our lives, hiding nothing, looking deeply into one another's hearts. Each one of us had come to a new relationship with the Lord Jesus and each one of us knew and knew that we knew. But as a result of this deep sharing something quite new happened between us; we each knew that the other fellow knew that we knew. We had become a team—we knew we were in something infinitely precious together, that He was giving us something for England. He had not only made us a team, but given us a vision for England. Had anyone asked us "What is your vision for England?" we could have told him. As a result, a river of blessing to flow from that little group—which river has become rivers, going on flowing in increasing depth and breadth. And that little team is no longer a little team; and an ever-growing number all over the country can share how Jesus has revived their ebbing spiritual experience and is doing new things in their lives. And this, many know, is the way

God has called forth His teams for revival in other countries around the world.

Perhaps the surest test of whether we are a team with another is whether we feel free to speak to him about the needs and lacks of a third party. If we were not a team, our sharing would be inhibited and we would fear lest it appear merely as an essay in criticism. But if we are a true team of the deep order mentioned above, it is then only out of love and concern for that one in order that we may make him great for Jesus and that we might pray and work to that end.

In those early days God brought to us a picture of teams of two for revival under the figure of a pair of sandals. We heard the Lord saying, "Will you just be My sandals for Me to walk in?" The sandals were not for show, or to be admired by others, but simply to be pressed into the dust under His feet, to take Him where He directed and into those lives which He desired to meet. But it was not to be merely a single sandal, but a pair of them— a team of two for revival. Let us go deep with but one other to begin with, and He can multiply the sandals over our respective lands beyond anything we could have thought.